AF404431

Andreas Herteux

First Foundations of Behavioral Capitalism

A New Variety of Capitalism Gains Power and Influence

Content

Introductory Remarks

The world is changing at breakneck speed. At no point can this be seen more clearly than in technological progress, which has seriously reshaped and often fundamentally changed social, political, economic and individual life. But this development is much more than just a small extension of the existing being. It changes this fundamentally and yet there doesn't seem to be enough description for this process and its commercial use. Are there only a few Internet companies that have completely new offers? Or is everything to be interpreted on a larger scale? Where does it lead to? What happens to the data and how is it used? How is profit generated with our behavior? Is there any possibility of manipulation here? Critical questions therefore do exist, but they remain piecemeal.

In sum, a feeling seems to have emerged for the fact that there is much more at stake than new business models and yet so far there has been no form of articulation, no descriptive structure that clearly states that we can no longer talk about the business conduct of individual companies, but that we already have to talk about a new variety of capitalism: Behavioral Capitalism. This capitalism rose with breathtaking speed and has become an integral part of many people's lives as it is closely linked to technological development. It offers opportunities, but also risks, since its power, in contrast to financial capitalism, which has also risen in the shadows, extends to the intimacy of the individual and is becoming more and more entrenched. For this reason it is of central importance to bring him out of the approximate and nebulous into the light, to name him clearly and to discuss him. So far, this has not been possible, except for individual pieces.

The Model of Behavioral Capitalism attempts to fill this gap and thus for the first time creates an order that makes a new variety of capitalism tangible and understandable. At the same time, this creates a basis for argumentation that is suitable for leaving the circles of experts and scholars and spreading them generally and comprehensibly, because the discussion about Behavioral Capitalism is not one that can only be conducted within small circles, certain milieus or in the feuilleton, but rather must become a central topic of the general public.

With this project we are still at the very beginning. But if we do not start, Behavioral Capitalism, analogous to financial capitalism, will work in the shadows and perhaps unfold a potential that can be used more for power and domination than for the good of mankind. In the light and with the help of public observation, it seems easier to steer the torrential river in the right direction than to hope childishly and naively that this will happen on its own. But we are still at the imaginary starting line with this thought.

Therefore, this paper primarily covers the previous publications on the topic of Behavioral Capitalism. These will therefore be printed as they have been published. Redundancy is therefore given, but undoubtedly also creates memory values.

These publications have given rise to initial discussions and questions, which are dealt with in a separate section.

It is therefore a documentation of an early phase that can serve as a printed reference work, but in no way claims to present the object of research conclusively and finally.

It should also be noted that Behavioral Capitalism will be a central topic of the 21st century, but remains only a part of it. An important one, but one that cannot be separated from elements such as the Milieu Struggle, the Irritant Society, the Change of Times and Collective Individualism for a coherent picture of present and future. Only an overall view is the key to a global understanding and thus to a comprehensive solution. Behavioral Capitalism is therefore an important explanatory pattern, but one that requires classification into a larger structure, which, however, will not be part of this writing.

Keeping this in mind may be difficult, due to the bisance and the dominance of the content of the individual sub-areas, since each could be the subject of a whole life as a researcher, but it is absolutely necessary, since otherwise it can come to one-sided misjudgements. This has to be avoided by the aforementioned overall view.

Andreas Herteux

Behavioral Capitalism - A New Variety of Capitalism Gains Power and Influence

- Human behaviour is a usable raw material

- This raw material has developed into a production factor due to technological progress.

- This production factor has led to new business models that now have a massive impact on economic, political and social life.

- It is therefore necessary to speak of a new variation of capitalism: Behavioral Capitalism.

- This new form of capitalism is not yet understood as such, which entails the danger that it creates power and market

relations that can hardly or only with great difficulty be corrected later.

The world is experiencing a change of times and an era of change. Dynamic, fast and at which point can this be recognized more clearly than by technological progress, which powerfully and at an incredible speed changes personal and community life and leaves almost no field untouched, be it politics, society or economy. Within the framework of this process, influence has shifted and new ones have been established. But all that almost imperceptibly, almost creepingly in the shadows and yet at the end almost all of it tangent. Technology more than ever means power and this special influence through the smart world, can be found today in the western world astonishingly bundled with a few companies, which naturally have little interest in explaining the risks of their activity too publicly, because they primarily see the opportunities of their actions and not the dangers. Who will blame them? How many people really understand their business models? Didn't they seem to come out of nowhere, these billion-dollar companies that are now indispensable?

This new influence of the large technology groups, which often exist only for a few years, is astonishing and astonishing, as is the development that their products have become an indispensable part of everyday life for many people and society at breakneck speed. A silent conquest and yet they are much more than just clever business models that can be easily integrated into the existing. These companies are only players on a playing field that has made their existence and growth possible in the first place. One thing that has too often been underestimated and overlooked so far is Behavioral Capitalism.

With this term, the child itself was derived and baptized by the author of these lines, the feeling for the shift of power relations gets an ordering, well-founded framework and becomes comprehensible. The accumulation of power can no longer hide behind the mechanisms of the new, but is clearly visible in the light. A necessity, because an unbridled and unbridled Behavioral Capitalism is even more dangerous than an angry financial capitalism, because it needs not only capital, but man as a whole to harvest. Anytime, any day. Yes, the phenomenon was palpable. Now it finds its analysis and order. Behavioral Capitalism must therefore be identified and interpreted in order to be able to deal with it self-confidently and positively. The wild horse needs dressage, otherwise it will go through at the end.

In isolated cases, and this should be noted, there are already further attempts to give the new era a verbalized form, of which in particular Shoshana Zuboff's concept of surveillance capitalism is to be mentioned, but this, and forgive me this word, does not go far enough to sufficiently explain the corresponding global changes and also concentrates strongly on possible negative aspects of a raging development, which can be both a blessing and a curse, the truth usually lies in the middle.

The model of Behavioral Capitalism therefore follows a different, neutral approach and has little in common with surveillance capitalism other than that both want to approach the same phenomenon. Nevertheless, it is recommended to work with this preparation. However, since these pages are only intended to briefly describe Behavioral Capitalism, a deeper examination of other concepts can only take place separately.

Let us therefore begin with the actual topic and immediately with a definition:

> **Behavioral Capitalism is a variant of capitalism in which human behaviour becomes the central factor for the production and provision of goods and services.**

The key to understanding this new form of capitalism is to look at human behavior as a usable resource.

From this, as far as it can be sufficiently won, on the one hand the needs of the people can be derived, but on the other hand also prognoses for future action. On the basis of this raw material, products and services can therefore be produced that correspond to the needs or future behaviour. It is also possible to trade the data itself on the market. How behavior is defined?

> **Behaviour means acting, tolerating as well as not acting. The processes can be conscious or unconscious. It is influenced and produced by stimuli.**

All of this may sound terribly abstract, but on closer inspection, behavior has always been used as a raw material, though not always so. We do not want to refer to the sale of indulgences in the Middle Ages, but to the insurance industry. It is a prime example of how the behaviour of the customer, often in the person of the representative, is researched, then evaluated by the company, and finally used to improve existing products, i.e. insurance, and to create new services. Only in this way were creative developments such as safeguarding one's own death conceivable. Since these are immaterial, i.e. intangible goods, the behaviour of interested parties and customers is of outstanding importance.

Basically, it has always been a production factor, at least in these areas, and it is with this very idea that we can approach this new form of capitalism, because the recognition that the needs and behaviour of potential customers are an important component of being able to offer and sell products and services effectively is neither original, nor does it require more in-depth study.

But now the conditions have changed, because technological development has led to new business models that have gained such an influence that they raise the question of whether they have long since developed into an independent form of capitalism, Behavioral Capitalism. This brings us to the central thesis of this paper, which is that new possibilities of behavioural skimming have turned the raw material into a factor of production and thus into a variant of capitalism in its own right.

The central production factor of Behavioral Capitalism is human behavior.

Not that one did not always want to know as much as possible, but only with the aforementioned techno-logical development did the problem of the difficult acquisition of behavioral data disappear into thin air within a very short time. It is therefore hardly surpri-sing at what speed large technology companies such as Amazon, Facebook or Google emerged and began to collect data, use behaviour according to capitalist me-thods and embed people bit by bit. Algorithms and automation made possible what humans would not have been able to do.

They were the great behavioral capitalists. Now they analyse the homo stimulus and try to generate in-formation or data on the basis of its behaviour or to offer or mediate products and services. Tailored to the individual. The raw material "behaviour" became a production factor.

This new factor of production is now so important that it has also become indispensable for classical and financial capitalism, since knowledge of current behaviour, composed of vast amounts of data obtained, makes it possible in many cases to assess or influence future behaviour.

Today, behaviour is also a central production factor for classical and financial capitalism and complements labour, land and capital.

This behaviour is then used directly as merchandise or processed into satisfaction and/or forecast products in a production process.

> **A <u>satisfaction product aims to</u> satisfy human needs.**
>
> **A <u>prognosis product</u> predicts future human behavior.**
>
> **<u>Behavioural data</u> can also be traded without further processing.**

Algorithms and more and more artificial intelligence take over this task. To simplify, we summarize this decentralized process in the descriptive metaphor of the behavioral factory.

> **The storage of behavior as well as the processing to satisfaction and prognosis products take place in the behavior factory.**

So much for the basic definitions and the history of development. In the following, the functionality and the value creation process of Behavioral Capitalism will be examined in more detail.

The Cycle of Behavioral Capitalism

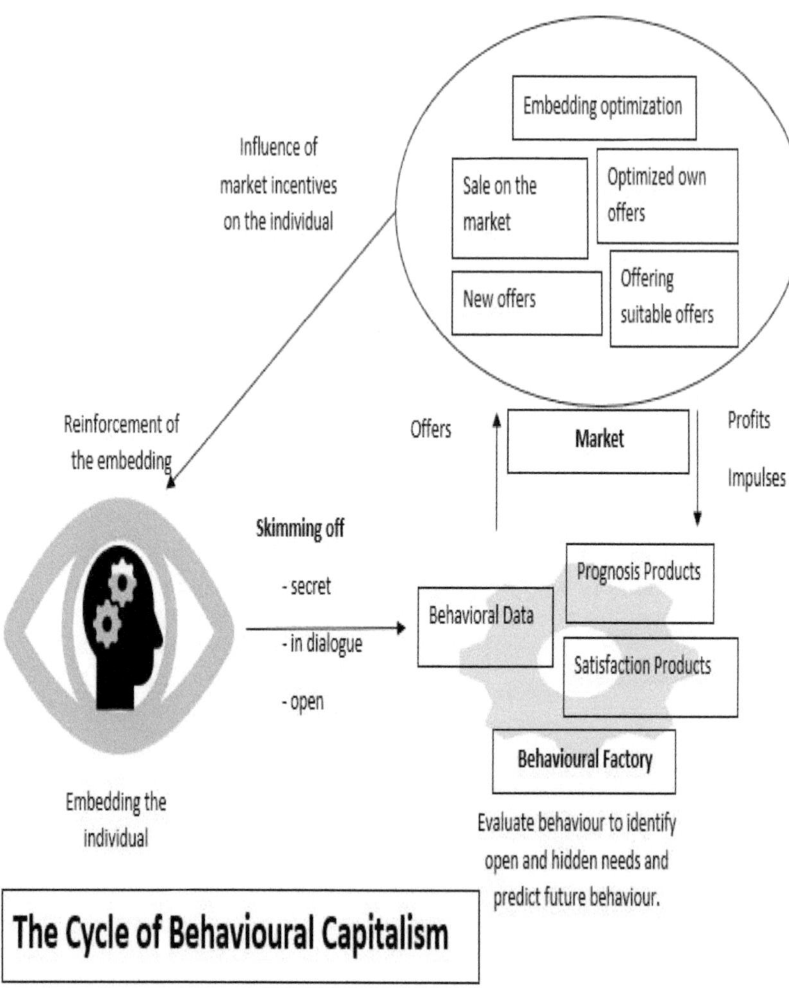

Absorption of behavioural data

Behavioral Capitalism is based on the raw material and production factor behaviour, which is created by the reaction of the individual to stimuli. He must first win this by skimming. There have always been such attempts, but it was the technological progress driven by the change of times that made automated harvesting in large quantities possible. The skimming process has three variants:

- **Open skimming**

    In this case, the individual is aware that his or her data will be used to produce certain corresponding forecast and satisfaction products.

    A typical example would be the input in a search engine. His personal behaviour or interest is used openly to present him with the desired result. In just one minute, for example, 2017 will be a worldwide event:

- 3.8 million Google searches

- 47,000 Instagram Photo Uploads

- 4.1 million Youtube video clicks

- 530,000 snap chat photo shares

- 456,000 Twitter message transmissions

These figures impressively prove that many behavioural data are transmitted voluntarily in many cases, because this creates added value for the user.

- **Dialogic skimming**

In the dialogical skimming off, the individual and a machine (algorithm, AI) enter into a dialogue process that serves not only to identify needs, but also to estimate future behavior. In doing so, both sides react to stimuli and it is now possible to disclose needs that the user may not have been aware of. The interaction can be open or hidden. What is important is that the process goes beyond an action.

- **Hidden skimming**

  With concealed skimming, the behaviour is harvested and further processed or resold without the knowledge of the user. An example would be when profile data of an individual is used in a social network to develop commercial products and services to use for behavior manipulation or control. The model case here would be the use of 87 million Facebook user data from Cambridge Analytica for the election campaign of Donald Trump in 2017.

The boundaries between the individual variants are of course fluid. For example, the majority of search engine users are now well aware that the results are accompanied by product ads from the same range of topics. Similarly, social media users should be aware that their data is being used for embedding. A rigid separation of the types of levy therefore makes little sense.

Transformation in the behavioural factory

The data volumes obtained are now stored in the behavioural factory, a metaphor to represent a complicated and decentralised processing process more plastically, and processed in parts into products. Forecast products as well as satisfaction products are produced.

Forecast products are used to estimate the future behaviour of an individual. A typical example would be a user of a social network who is interested in hiking, presents photos and documents participation in events. The algorithm can now read this data and supplement it with other information such as age, place of residence, brand inclinations, style, etc. The algorithm can also read the data from the data. Paired with the reading of the browser history, which can happen even if you are no longer logged in to the corresponding network, a forecast product is created, the result of which could be, for example, that exactly this user is highly likely to set off on the corresponding tours again in summer. It would therefore make sense to virtually confront him with suitable services (e.g. travel offers) or products (e.g. hiking boots) shortly beforehand. The forecast product opens the door for a targeted approach.

Satisfaction products, on the other hand, are specifically aimed at satisfying identified needs. Not in the future, but in the present. It is interesting to note that a satisfaction product can refer both to a need that the user is aware of and to a need that he has not yet reflected on, but which results from the analysis of behaviour. Thus, it is precisely satisfaction products, but also prognosis products, that have the function of revealing the inner needs of the individual and can thus be an important element of self-realization.

Trading on the market

Both prognosis and satisfaction products as well as the behaviour itself can be used or sold by the data collector himself. This generates massive profits, which are usually reinvested. Not necessarily only in the previous business model, but also in other fields that invite networking. The following opportunities therefore arise for the market:

- **Offering suitable offers**

    The data is used to offer suitable offers to the individual. This can consist of own services and products, combined, however, these are usually with the advertisement for third parties. The core of the business model can still be seen here today.

    Overall, it is estimated that 25% of global advertising revenues are now generated by Facebook and Google, two of the best examples of applied Behavioral Capitalism. By 2016, it was still 20%. Tendency rising.

- **New offers**

  Behaviour makes it necessary to design entirely new products in order to satisfy the needs identified from them. The idea of deriving the necessary innovations and further developments from market observation is as old as economic activity itself, but thanks to the new possibilities of siphoning off a raw material that was previously difficult to extract, it has reached a completely new dimension.

- **Optimization of own offers**

  The own offers are improved and adapted by behavior products and appropriate feedback. This applies both to the collectors of the data and to their customers. In particular, the learning machine relies on these reactions to constantly improve its functions.

- **Sale on the market**

  The data volumes are made available to third parties raw or already as processing products for their own business activities.

- **embedding optimization**

  The collective individualism knows the embedding of man the creation of an individual reality. Behavioral Capitalism contributes to this through a continuous cycle of behavioural skimming.

Embedding process

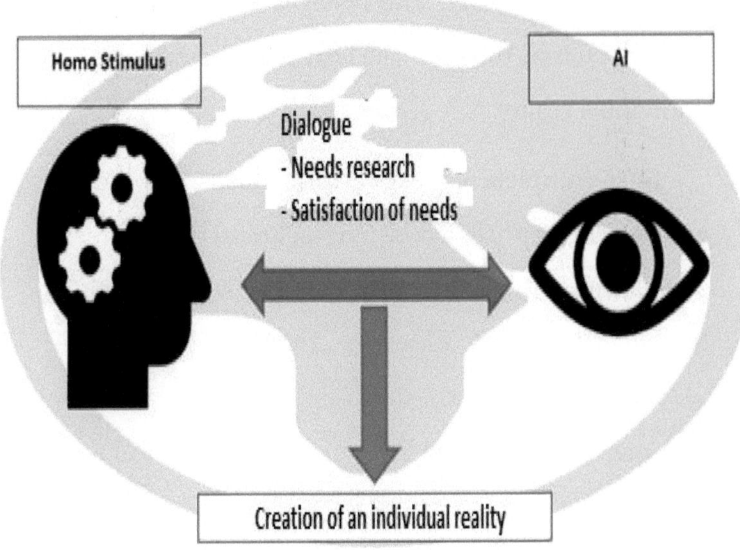

Stimulation of the individual to react

In the ideal case, the individual reacts to the stimuli offered and thus creates new behaviour, which in turn can be skimmed off. The result is a cycle of embedding, which in the end can lead to the creation of an individual reality.

In a complete collective individualism, which of course presupposes a constant technical development, the skimmed-off would now sink bit by bit into an individualized reality. However, this is still incomplete due to the presence of milieu fights. At the same time, the raw material behavior and the investment capital accumulate, which further improves the possibilities of the behavior factory and skimming. A cycle develops. The game, driven by the machine, starts from the beginning. Thus, on the one hand, it causes the embedding of man, but at the same time it also causes the further drifting apart of the social milieus.

Inventory and outlook

Behavioral Capitalism is a variant of capitalism that, like financial capitalism, is difficult to identify in its effects and therefore plays only a subordinate role in public perception and on the political agenda. He cleverly uses this to spread and consolidate himself, which in capitalism is often characterized by the emergence of monopolies or oligopolies. This is impressively demonstrated by the real situation of the technology groups and their market power.

Behavioral Capitalism has therefore become firmly established, but without being perceived as such. State-of-the-art technology enables a never-before-seen embedding that can penetrate into the most intimate areas of the individual. A development that requires closer scrutiny and must not continue to take place in the shadows, for an unleashed Behavioral Capitalism would be an even stronger force than financial capitalism ever was. He would be a means of domination.

The presentation of this development was deliberately neutral, as it entails both opportunities and risks. The embedding of the individual in his own world, which serves his own fulfilment of needs and self-realisation, is at first not negative, especially since this does not have to be designed in a closed way. On the other hand, of course, there is a central world of who ultimately controls the stimuli and the data and whether the behavior or even one's own reality is manipulated. This, like the model of Behavioral Capitalism, is now to be released for discussion.

This paper is available under DOI 10.13140/RG.2.2.18058.62402 and has been published several times in the same form and in German and English and released for discussion. In Germany, for example, in the weekly newspaper "Der Freitag":

https://www.freitag.de/autoren/aherteux/der-auf-

stieg-des-verhaltenskapitalismus

Behavioral Capitalism - Rise in the Shadow

interview

Andreas Herteux, the founder of the Erich von Werner Society on the functioning and increasing influence of Behavioral Capitalism, which he researched, analyzed and identified.

Mr. Herteux, you have described a new type of capitalism. How would you describe it in a few words?

Behavioral Capitalism is a variant of capitalism in which human behaviour becomes the central factor for the production and provision of goods and services.

Sounds very abstract at first.

This is true and it also makes it very difficult to recognize Behavioral Capitalism at all. Actually, it's not that hard. Let's think of a baker and his buns. It should be clear to all of us what raw materials he will need for the production process. For our buns, maybe flour, water, yeast and some salt. Let's jump from the bakery to the Internet. Most of us have already encountered personalized advertising. For example, we have been looking for a holiday in the mountains and suddenly we are confronted with emails, banner ads and social media reports on the subject. However, this personalised advertising can only be addressed to us if our behaviour, in this case the search query, has been evaluated beforehand. All the services, advertisements, suggestions for friendship - all these rolls were baked from one dough: our behaviour that was previously open, concealed or skimmed off in dialogue and then evaluated, which means that this raw material was transformed into prognosis and satisfaction products in a metaphorical behavioural factory in order to get something individual for us from the metaphorical oven.

If you look at it from the point of view, is behavior the flour of Internet companies?

Right, human behaviour is therefore obviously a usable raw material and this raw material has developed through technological progress into a production factor, which has led to completely new business models, which in the meantime have a massive influence on economic, political and social life. It would be fatal to speak of just one business model here, because its power is far too great for that. Rather, it is a new variation of capitalism: Behavioral Capitalism.

Is the use of human behaviour really a new phenomenon?

Of course, human behaviour has always been an essential factor and raw material. Already alone for the areas of sales and marketing, but also as raw material. Let us just think here of the insurance industry, which had already skimmed "behaviour" from customers long before the modern age and thus designed new products and optimised old ones. In this industry, this raw material has always been more and more a primary basis for business. By the way, also in politics or, if you like it historically, in the sale of indulgences. However, technical progress has almost infinitely increased the possibility of behavioural skimming and they no longer need a human being for evaluation, but, to put it simply, only the learning machine. Just two numbers to underline this; Google alone had about 3.8 million searches by 2017 and Youtube 4.1 million video clicks. Per minute. You can calculate approximately how much behavioural data can be skimmed off in one day and for the most part a product or service can even be produced and offered immediately, even if it is only the answer to a search query.

My insurance agent can only dream of such amounts of data.

Insurance companies are much better positioned today, but you can see the difference in the right place. Only a change of times, the elements of which also include the rapid and dynamic development of technology and the conditioning of man to its use, which would be described as an irritant society, whereby we do not want to drift into psychology, have turned a raw material into a production factor. So today we can speak of Behavioral Capitalism.

Is there a parallel for such a development? Yes, according to a similar principle, financial capitalism has outgrown classical capitalism. Although capital has always been an economic factor of production, it was only much too late to realize that it had led as an independent element to a new variety of capitalism. Even today, there are major problems in recognizing and correctly interpreting its mechanisms. That's why he can act a little under the radar. Here there is a parallel to Behavioral Capitalism.

Sohsana Zuboff also warns of the dangers of such a development, although she does not use the term "Behavioral Capitalism" that you coined, but speaks of surveillance capitalism.

Yes and I appreciate her meticulous and critical work very much, but her concept of surveillance capitalism has little in common with the model of Behavioral Capitalism. Mrs. Zuboff sees her surveillance capitalism, and the word already betrays this, as something fundamentally negative and man-made, which a few people a few years ago came up with at Google to consciously gain power, wealth and influence. For Behavioral Capitalism, on the other hand, development is a logical consequence of capitalism and is in continuity. It is not a degeneration, as she calls it, but the water simply flows on. Companies like Google emerged from this river and not outside it somewhere on the dry bank.

Nevertheless, both of you were faced with the dangers.

It is true, however, surveillance capitalism views the development exclusively negatively. He wants to warn, wants to be subjective and not necessarily show a model as a representation of reality. Behavioral Capitalism wants exactly that, therefore weighs up opportunities and risks and strives for a neutral presentation of general mechanisms. Of course, he also sees the possibilities of manipulation, but also the other side.

Just think of our example of search queries. You will also receive an answer from Google & Co. and Youtube will show you the desired video. Personalised content does not have to be fundamentally bad, even if it is concealed, because with embedding it may even be possible to identify needs that people would never have discovered without the new technology. Just take the example of a holiday in the mountains. Perhaps the learning machine works out for you that mountaineering has always been your passion? Would that be bad if you discovered such an inner need?

On the downside there is of course also the possibility of manipulation. We must defend ourselves against them, but we must not deceive ourselves, as much as we want to. Larger sections of the population, i.e. not a few milieus, will gladly exchange part of their freedom for an embedding that determines their needs and satisfies them. Perhaps some homo stimulus even get the possibilities of self-development for the first time. That sounds frightening to some ears, but it will be reality. But resignation would be the wrong reaction. Rather, reality should encourage us to make it clear to everyone that they do not have to choose: embedding or freedom, but can have both. But there are not even any signs of this. A very dangerous situation.

How should one confront the dangers of Behavioral Capitalism?

First of all by recognizing them and placing them in the right context. Behavioral Capitalism, together with the stimulus society, will trigger an era of collective individualism, in which the process of individualization will, however, be hampered by milieu struggles. Fundamental points with which we at the Erich von Werner Society deal in depth, because here is also the cause of the difficult social situation to see and not in obsolete explanatory models from the previous century such as the outdated left-right scheme.

This and the fact that we are on the threshold of a new era that will radically change the international balance of power in the coming decades must be realized and accepted. Something's moving. Even if we were to recognize this, we would need ideas and here we have unfortunately become very unimaginative or capitulate to a complex world and so many interrelationships, so we need a comprehensive solution that can solve all these problems. With the model of alternative hegemony (AH model) we have presented such a model that could correct capitalism and meet the great challenges of our time. With it we can transform capitalism into a value market economy.

Change for the better is therefore possible. All it takes is courage.

The interview was published in German and English in various media. For example, it is available here: https://www.dailypress.com/dp-ugc-article-behavioral-capitalism-andreas-herteux-on-th-2-2019-09-18-story.html

Behavioral Capitalism and Surveillance Capitalism - A Comparison of Two Interpretations of a Development of Capitalism

- Behavioral Capitalism regards the absorption and use of behavioural data as a logical capitalist further development in historical continuity and thus as an inevitable development.

- Surveillance capitalism distinguishes between behaviour that is needed to optimise existing services and data that is not needed for them. He considers the use of "excess behaviour" as an explicitly man-made, non-compulsory and degenerate form of capitalism, the ultimate goal of which is the accumulation of power, wealth and influence.

- Behaviour has always been a raw material for Behavioral Capitalism, which has become a production factor through technical development.

- In surveillance capitalism, the so-called "surplus behaviour" was discovered by Google and exploited free of charge by this and other companies.

- Behavioral Capitalism sees both the opportunities and the risks of this development.

- Surveillance capitalism, on the other hand, is interpreted exclusively negatively.

- Behavioral Capitalism stands in a context from which it cannot be torn, and knowledge of these connections is indispensable for dealing with it and understanding it.

- Surveillance capitalism is an isolated construct, ultimately created a few years ago, whose authorship can be found among others at Google and can therefore also be combated in this way.

Introductory remarks

Within a very short period of time, technological development has made new business models possible, shifted power relations and, in the end, created a new form of capitalism. This development is often viewed critically, but so far this debate still lacks a structure and models with which a targeted and also simple classification can take place as a basis for a broad discussion. There are already first attempts to establish these and two interpretations of this evolution will be dealt with in the following.

These are the concept of surveillance capitalism and the model of Behavioral Capitalism. Different approaches to be contrasted in order to show that we are not talking about the establishment of new business models, but about a new form of capitalism that requires our full attention, since it risks exerting a serious influence on social, societal, political and economic life that reaches into the most intimate realm of the individual. This power cannot and must not hide in the shadows, but must be part of a public discussion that would be greatly facilitated by a structured presentation of this development of capitalism.

The main features of surveillance capitalism were presented by Shoshana Zuboff in her book "The Age of Surveillance Capitalism".[1] This work serves as the primary basis for the discussion and comparisons between the concept of surveillance capitalism and that of Behavioral Capitalism. With regard to the methodology, it should also be noted that quotations and thus also the page numbers refer to the German version of the work.[2] This is justified by the fact that the book was first published in German and that a large

---

[1] Zuboff, Shoshana, The Age of Surveillance Capitalism: The Fight for the Future at the New Frontier of Power Profile Books; 31. 01.2019

[2] Zuboff, Shoshana, The Age of Surveillance Capitalism. Campus Publishing House 4 October 2018; 04 October 2018

number of supplementary interviews or reports are available.[3] Any meetings held in English, however, have been included in the overall assessment in the same way as the non-English ones.

On the other hand, own research results are presented, the publication of which, however, is still of a more recent nature and still has to go the way of establishment and acceptance.

The aims of this writing are therefore:

1) To compare two fundamental interpretations of the development of capitalism

2) To contribute to making this new phenomenon describable and giving it a mediable structure

---

[3] It is acknowledged that minor differences are possible in the back-translation into English.

3) To create a basis for discussion on the opportunities and risks of capitalist development.

It should be noted from the outset that the author of this paper is also the author of the treatises on Behavioral Capitalism.

1. Definitions and origin

Shosana Zuboff summarizes the modern development in capitalism under the term "surveillance capitalism". It offers a longer definition for this, which is to be considered step by step and compared with that of Behavioral Capitalism:

> *"[...] [Surveillance capitalism is] a new market form that claims human experience as a free raw material for its hidden commercial operations of extraction, forecasting and sale."*[4]

In surveillance capitalism, man ultimately plays the role of a field that is harvested by the technology companies in order to earn money with the products won in the end, as well as to gain power and influence.

---

[4] The definition is to be found in the introduction and therefore has no separate page number.

Parallel to this, it is pointed out that surveillance capitalism can be described as a new market form through its influence on social, personal, social, political and economic life.

This should be contrasted with the definition of Behavioral Capitalism, which has some similarities and many more differences:

> *"Behavioral Capitalism is a variant of capitalism in which human behaviour becomes the central factor in the production and provision of goods and services.*[5]

The definition of Behavioral Capitalism is broader because it focuses only on the rank of "behaviour" as a factor of production. However, Behavioral Capitalism also assumes that this is a new form of capitalism. Both models therefore agree on this point. An interesting difference, however, is that it focuses on human

---

[5] Herteux, Andreas, Behavioural Capitalism - A New Variety of Capitalism Gains Power and Influence

behaviour rather than experience. The behavior is defined as follows:

> *"Behaviour is understood as acting, tolerating as well as not acting. The*
>
> *Processes can be conscious or unconscious. It is influenced and produced by stimuli.* [...] **The** *central production factor of Behavioral Capitalism is human behavior."*[6]

Whether it is, however, only a linguistic blur must remain open, in the graphic overview ("The Discovery of the Surplus of Behaviour"; page 121) in Zuboff's book, experience is no longer mentioned. The terms may be understood synonymously here.

In Behavioral Capitalism, on the other hand, behavior is deliberately spoken of because it is based on the

---

[6] Herteux, Andreas, Behavioural Capitalism - A New Variety of Capitalism Gains Power and Influence

theory of the stimulus society, which assumes a development into a homo stimulus.[7]

The origin of surveillance capitalism

The differences become clearer when looking at the broader definition of surveillance capitalism. Zuboff[8] describes this as *"a form of capitalism cut out of its kind, characterized by a concentration of wealth, knowledge and power unparalleled in human history"*.

---

[7] Herteux Andreas, Die Reizgesellschaft - On the way to the age of collective individualism;
"A stimulus society is generally understood to be an association of individuals who are exposed to stimuli which influence a strong frequency, which are usually artificially generated, and who have difficulty or are unable to resist these stimuli, or in some cases do not wish to resist them. [...] The homo stimulus, the stimulus man, emerges."

[8] The definition is to be found in the introduction and therefore has no separate page number.

Surveillance capitalism is not only an anomaly, however, but was consciously created by a few people at the beginning of the recent past and used to constantly increase its own power:

> *"Surveillance capitalism begins with the discovery of the surplus of behaviour [...] Above all,[9] we must keep one thing in mind: Surveillance capitalism was invented by a specific group of people, at a specific time, in a specific place. It is not necessarily the result of either digital technology or information capitalism. He was consciously created [...][10]*

> *"Google had achieved its first successes in the online business at the beginning of the 2000s and then forecast click rates for tailor-*

---

[9] Page 121

[10] Zuboff, page 108

made ads. But monitoring is no longer limited to online advertising. The products created by surveillance are becoming increasingly more lucrative than traditional products and services. Companies from all walks of life compete for our behavioral data so they can predict what, when, and how we will act, feel, want, and buy."[11]

"Surveillance capitalism is a historical phenomenon, not a technological inevitability. It was invented around 2001 by a company called Google."[12]

---

[11] Interview with the Süddeutsche Zeitung of 07.11.2018; https://www.sueddeutsche.de/digital/shoshana-zuboff-ueberwachungskapitalismus-google-facebook-1.4198835

[12] Interview with the weekly magazine "Der Freitag" from 02.04.2019; https://www.freitag.de/autoren/the-guardian/tyrannei-die-sich-von-menschen-ernaehrt

It is therefore only understandable if surveillance capitalism is ultimately viewed negatively, for it is the

> *"[...] parasitic [...] foundation and framework of a surveillance economy [...] the origin of a new instrumental power that claims above society and confronts market democracy with disturbing challenges.[...] aims at a new collective order on the basis of total certainty.[...] an expropriation of critical human rights that can best be understood as a coup from above - the overthrow of popular sovereignty."[13]*

The origin of Behavioral Capitalism

In contrast to surveillance capitalism, Behavioral Capitalism sees the developments in capitalism not as

---

[13] The definition is to be found in the introduction and therefore has no separate page number.

a man-made plan, but as a logical and compelling further development of capitalism itself.

Not Google & Co. have developed a business model, but the change of times has[14] opened up a new direction for capitalism, which was only taken by the technology companies.

It was therefore not necessary for any company to discover any form of behaviour in the back room, but behaviour has always been a raw material. A prime example of this is the insurance industry, which researched, evaluated and used customer behavior long before the Internet age to optimize current insurance products and generate new ones. Basically, it has always been a production factor, at least in these areas, and it is with this very idea that we can approach this new form of capitalism, because the recognition that the needs and behaviour of potential customers are an important component of being able to offer and sell

---

[14] Herteux Andreas, Concept of Time Change

products and services effectively is neither original, nor does it require more in-depth study.

But through new technologies, the establishment of the irritant society and the possibilities of machine skimming, a small tributary stream arose from the rapid main stream of capitalism, which in time also developed into a dangerous body of water. An evolution that we already experienced with financial capitalism. Here, too, capital was an important means from the very beginning, but later broke away and founded an independent variety of capitalism. The fruit had grown on the tree, but the seed fell to the ground and grew there at an amazing rate. It is therefore hardly surprising at what speed large technology companies such as Amazon, Facebook or Google emerged and began to collect data as soon as the possibilities arose. So it was only logical to use behaviour according to capitalist methods and to embed people bit by bit. Algorithms and automation made possible what people would not have been able to do and the raw material and mere means of production became the production factor of

a new capitalism: Behavioral Capitalism.

56

Development of the varieties of capitalism

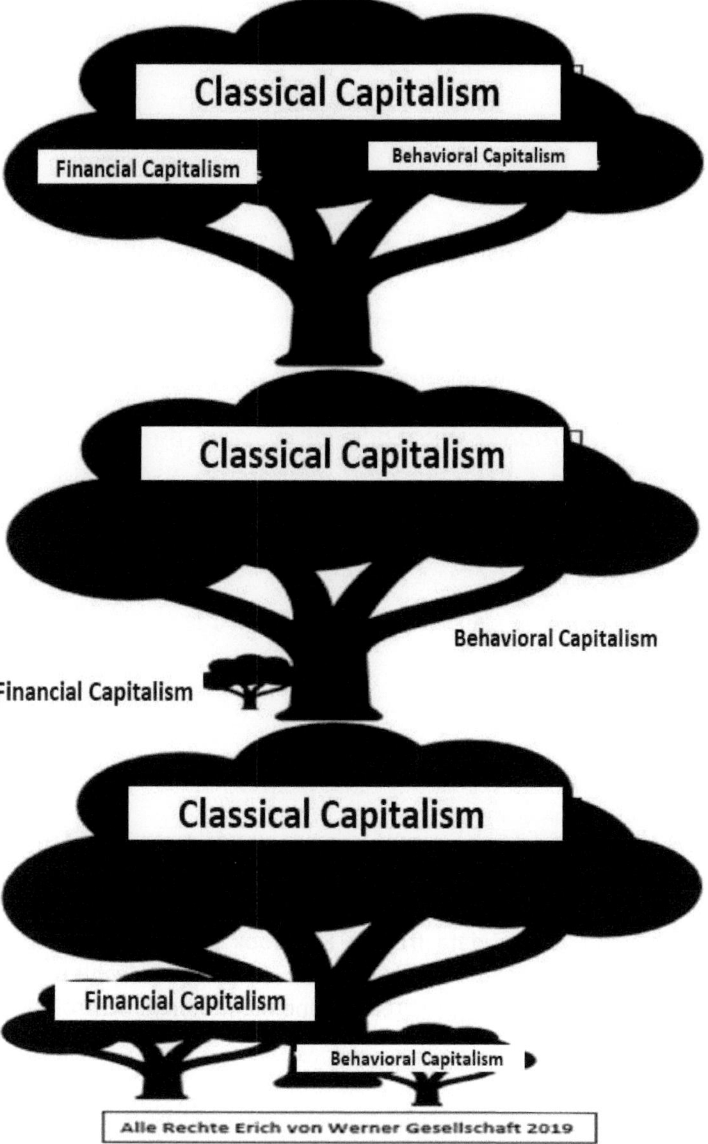

Classical Capitalism
Financial Capitalism
Behavioral Capitalism
Classical Capitalism
Behavioral Capitalism
Financial Capitalism
Classical Capitalism
Financial Capitalism
Behavioral Capitalism

2.   How it works

After considering definition and origin, the functionalities of both descriptions are now to be compared.

Surveillance Capitalism

Zuboff explains the functioning of surveillance capitalism as follows:

"Surveillance capitalism claims one-sided human experience as a raw material for transformation into behavioral data [...]"[15]

At this point it is assumed that surveillance capitalism, which is ultimately only the tool less, is used to siphon off experience without human consideration.[16]

---

[15] Zuboff, page 22

[16] A certain problem arises here again, through the use of the vague term "human experience". Is "experience" skimmed off by entering a term in a search engine? Or just the behavior, the input. When data from a Facebook profile is used to evaluate it, are empirical values used? No, ultimately it is only the input behavior when creating and maintaining the profile.

A very important point, because in the idea of surveillance capitalism the individual is merely the cow in the stable, which is constantly milked and in the end, metaphorically with the loss of freedom, slaughtered. Objections, such as that the person who enters a search query receives a list of results in return or that a concealed skimming could also serve to identify needs, are not accepted.

> *"It is difficult to determine our actual position in this constellation. First, we were told how happy we could be to get free services. When we found out that the companies were collecting data about us, we were "the product". And we were told this was a fair trade. But we are not the product, but rather the source, the freely accessible raw material. This in turn is processed into products that*

serve the interests of those who benefit from our future behavior."[17]

"They declared that they had the right to acquire our private experience, to transform it into data in order to own it as private property. Google began to claim unilaterally that the World Wide Web belonged to him and his search engine. [...] Once we searched Google, now Google searches us. We used to think digital services were freely available, now surveillance capitalists think we are freely available."[18]

---

[17] Interview with the Süddeutsche Zeitung of 07.11.2018; https://www.sueddeutsche.de/digital/shoshana-zuboff-ueberwachungskapitalismus-google-facebook-1.4198835

[18] Interview with the weekly magazine "Der Freitag" from 02.04.2019; https://www.freitag.de/autoren/the-guardian/tyrannei-die-sich-von-menschen-ernaehrt

Surveillance capitalism therefore not only interprets the relationship between surveillance capitalists and users as one-sided and parasitic, but also clearly warns against a further aggravation of this imbalance:

> *"But also because such a parasitic development has become the basis for a lucrative capitalism of the 21st century. There is now an unprecedented concentration of knowledge and power, free from democratic control and beyond our individual control. Surveillance capitalism is based on historically unimaginable knowledge asymmetries. Surveillance capitalists know all about us. We know very little of what they do or what they know. They use their knowledge advantage*

to influence our behaviour. It's a whole new kind of power.[19]

After the levies have been levied, the data obtained is divided:

> *"Some of this data is used to improve products and services, the rest is declared a proprietary surplus of behaviour from which, with the help of advanced manufacturing processes, which [...]* can be summarized under the *term "machines or artificial intelligence", prediction products are produced that anticipate what they will do now, in the near future, or sometime in the future. Finally, these forecasting products are traded*

---

[19] Interview with the Süddeutsche Zeitung of 07.11.2018; https://www.sueddeutsche.de/digital/shoshana-zuboff-ueberwachungskapitalismus-google-facebook-1.4198835

on a new type of behavioural forecasting marketplace, [...] [called] the behavioural futures market.[20]

At this point it becomes somewhat blurred, as it is not always clearly distinguished whether surveillance capitalism21 describes only the use of what is called "new means of production" or also that of improvement. The wording should refer to both.

The question of whether it is not one of the fundamental characteristics of capitalist economy that new products, services and innovations are generated from surpluses of means of production is left open. The same applies to the consideration of whether the identification of needs and requirements, which is ultimately nothing more than market research by modern means, does not have to be the business basis of every

---

[20] Zuboff, page 22

[21] Zuboff, page 121

company that cannot operate on a seller's market, under state protection or in an oligopoly or monopoly.

The separation also causes problems precisely because Zubuff in particular sees those data that are not required for optimization, i.e. the "behavior surplus", particularly critically:

> "More behavioral data is rendered than is necessary to improve the service. This surplus provides a new means of production that produces predictions from user behavior. These products are sold to business customers on new behavioural futures contracts. The behavioral value reinvestment cycle is subject to this new logic.[22]

But is it not the case that the data used for optimization and prediction should not be largely identical? And who are the new products for? For business

---

[22] Zuboff, page 121

customers only? Not for the customer himself? And isn't the market much bigger than described here? It seems a bit like trying to differentiate between good new capitalism ("optimization of services") and bad new capitalism ("use and generation of behavioural surpluses"), but does this differentiation really make sense?

These questions may be irrelevant if one wants to represent only an exploitation mechanism created outside the capitalist norm, for the purpose of accumulating power, influence and wealth of a few, but they become relevant when an overall structure of a new capitalism is sought, and that is precisely the aim of this paper: Making the inconspicuous visible in the shadows and generally understandable.

Behavioral Capitalism

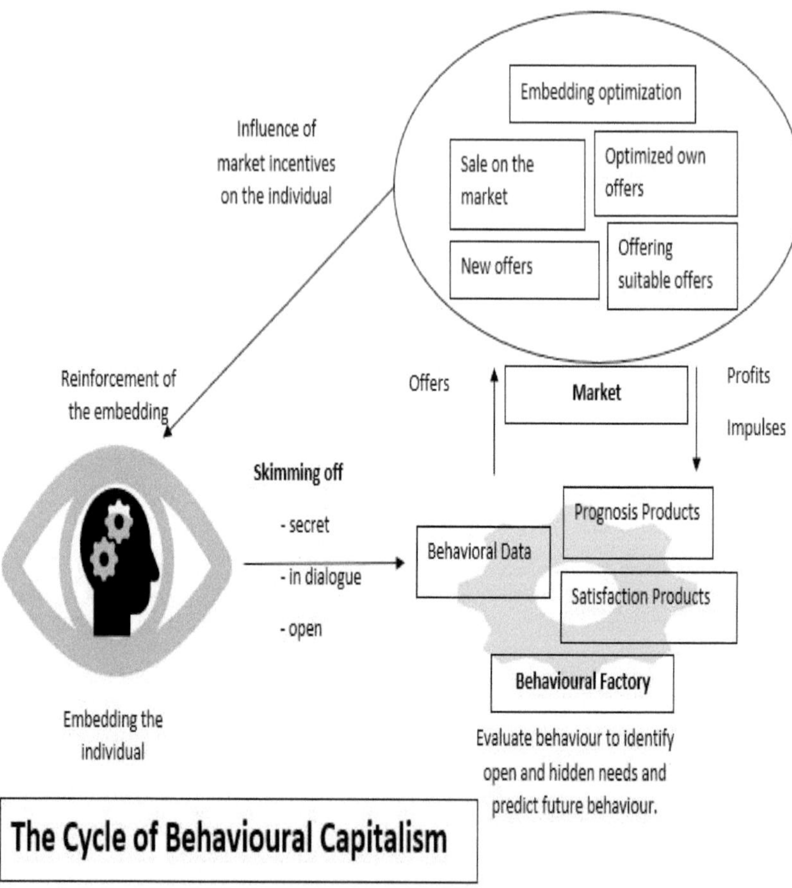

The Cycle of Behavioural Capitalism

Absorption of behavioural data

> **Today, behaviour is also a central production factor for classical and financial capitalism and complements labour, land and capital.**

Behavioral Capitalism is based on the raw material and production factor behaviour, which is created by the reaction of the individual to stimuli. He must first win this by skimming. There have always been such attempts, but it was the technological progress driven by the change of times that made automated harvesting in large quantities possible. The skimming process has three variants whose transitions can be fluid:

- **Open skimming**

- **Dialogic skimming**

- **Hidden skimming**

Transformation in the behavioural factory

The data volumes obtained are now stored in the behavioural factory, a metaphor to represent a complicated and decentralised processing process more plastically, and processed in parts into products. Forecast products as well as satisfaction products are produced.

> **A <u>satisfaction product aims to</u> satisfy human needs.**
>
> **A <u>prognosis product</u> predicts future human behavior.**
>
> **<u>Behavioural data</u> can also be traded without further processing.**

Forecast products are used to estimate the future behaviour of an individual. A typical example would be a user of a social network who is interested in hiking, presents photos and documents participation in events. The algorithm can now read this data and supplement it with other information such as age, place of residence, brand inclinations, style, etc. The algorithm can also read the data from the data. Paired with the reading of the browser history, which can happen even if you are no longer logged in to the corresponding network, a forecast product is created, the result of which could be, for example, that exactly this user is highly likely to set off on the corresponding tours again in summer. It would therefore make sense to virtually confront him with suitable services (e.g. travel offers) or products (e.g. hiking boots) shortly beforehand. The forecast product opens the door for a targeted approach.

Satisfaction products, on the other hand, are specifically aimed at satisfying identified needs. Not in the future, but in the present. It is interesting to note that a satisfaction product can refer both to a need that the user is aware of and to a need that he has not yet reflected on, but which results from the analysis of behaviour. Thus, it is precisely satisfaction products, but also prognosis products, that have the function of revealing the inner needs of the individual and can thus be an important element of self-realization.

Trading on the market

Both prognosis and satisfaction products as well as the behaviour itself can be used or sold by the data collector himself. This generates massive profits, which are usually reinvested. Not necessarily only in the previous business model, but also in other fields that invite networking. The following opportunities therefore arise for the market:

- **Offering suitable offers**

    The data is used to offer suitable offers to the individual. This can consist of own services and products, combined, however, these are usually with the advertisement for third parties. The core of the business model can still be seen here today.

Overall, it is estimated that 25% of global advertising revenues are now generated by Facebook and Google, two of the best examples of applied Behavioral Capitalism. By 2016, it was still 20%. Tendency rising.

- **New offers**

  Behaviour makes it necessary to design entirely new products in order to satisfy the needs identified from them. The idea of deriving the necessary innovations and further developments from market observation is as old as economic activity itself, but thanks to the new possibilities of siphoning off a raw material that was previously difficult to extract, it has reached a completely new dimension.

- **Optimization of own offers**

  The own offers are improved and adapted by behavior products and appropriate feedback. This applies both to the collectors of the data and to their customers. In particular, the learning machine relies on these reactions to constantly improve its functions.

- **Sale on the market**

  The data volumes are made available to third parties raw or already as processing products for their own business activities.

- **embedding optimization**

  The collective individualism knows the embedding of man the creation of an individual reality. Behavioral Capitalism contributes to this through a continuous cycle of behavioural skimming.

Embedding process

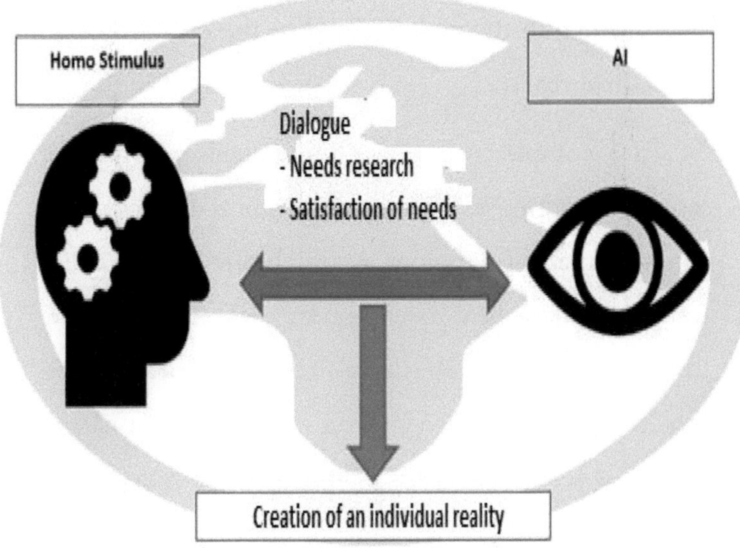

Stimulation of the individual to react

In the ideal case, the individual reacts to the stimuli offered and thus creates new behaviour, which in turn can be skimmed off. The result is a cycle of embedding, which in the end can lead to the creation of an individual reality.

In a complete collective individualism, which of course presupposes a constant technical development, the skimmed-off would now sink bit by bit into an individualized reality. However, this is still incomplete due to the presence of milieu fights. At the same time, the raw material behavior and the investment capital accumulate, which further improves the possibilities of the behavior factory and skimming. A cycle develops. The game, driven by the machine, starts from the beginning. Thus, on the one hand, it causes the embedding of man, but at the same time it also causes the further drifting apart of the social milieus.

3.   consideration

Behavioral Capitalism is a variant of capitalism that, like financial capitalism, is difficult to identify in its effects and therefore plays only a subordinate role in public perception and on the political agenda. He cleverly uses this to spread and consolidate himself, which in capitalism is often characterized by the emergence of monopolies or oligopolies. This is impressively demonstrated by the real situation of the technology groups and their market power.

Behavioral Capitalism has therefore become firmly established, but without being perceived as such. State-of-the-art technology enables a never-before-seen embedding that can penetrate into the most intimate areas of the individual. A development that requires closer scrutiny and must not continue to take place in the shadows, for an unleashed Behavioral Capitalism would be an even stronger force than financial capitalism ever was. He would be a means of domination.

The last two paragraphs could have been written in a similar, if not identical, way about the concept of surveillance capitalism, but the difference below the surface is unmistakable, because while surveillance capitalism views development as something abnormal, man-made and ultimately - unilaterally - evil that gives birth to even the worst, the portrayal of Behavioral Capitalism is deliberately neutral because it recognizes that it is a normal development of capitalism and offers both opportunities and risks. Zuboff's work presents the challenges in an excellent and meticulous manner; perhaps more convincingly than ever before. Not the odds. These are even denied.

The step-by-step embedding of the individual in his own world is at the same time a possibility not only to fulfil needs, but also to identify them. However, this process cannot be separated from the capitalist process, as Zuboff suggests. He needs the innovations and optimizations.

It also overlooks an important detail: the population of a country is divided into milieus, which are also decaying more and more quickly, some of which have completely different views, values or lifestyles. A considerable part of these milieus would always be willing to exchange elements such as democracy or freedoms that are not perceived for an embedding that satisfies their needs.

This realization may be frightening and yet it describes the facts. If Zuboff is therefore of *"be sand in the wheel"*[23], the *"unwillingness of citizens and journalists [...] the scientists [...] the elected representatives of the people and political decision-makers [...] and the young [r] people [...]",* then the *"unwillingness of the people and journalists [...] the scientists [...] the politicians [...] and the young [r] people [...]".* If we[24] speak of a general feeling of

---

[23]Zuboff, page 593

[24] Zuboff, page 596

"indignation"[25]that should develop, it should be noted that this will only be in the interest of part of the population.

But that is only a problem as long as development is seen as an isolated monstrosity that would be controlled with a rifle and whip. In fact, Behavioral Capitalism is not only in historical continuity, but is itself only a part of a transition into an era of collective individualism that, together with milieu struggles and the shifting of global power relations, will shape the future.

The idea that these great forces of change can be countered with some restrictions in the business activities of Western technology companies seems interesting, but it is not very purposeful, because wouldn't that mean that the field will ultimately be left to Baidu, Tencent, Alibaba & Co, often backed by the authority

----

[25] Zuboff, page 595

of the Chinese state? This is an important issue that needs to be discussed:

The dark sides of Behavioral Capitalism are a gigantic problem, but aren't we perhaps leaving the market to much more dangerous forces if we weaken Western corporations while we can't influence Eastern ones? It therefore requires a comprehensive solution concept, as we find it in the model of alternative hegemony (AH model), which should not be an issue here.

Towards the end

This writing finally dealt with:

1) To compare two fundamental interpretations of the development of capitalism

2) To contribute to making this new phenomenon describable and giving it a mediable structure

3) To create a basis for discussion on the opportunities and risks of capitalist development.

Shoshana Zubuff has succeeded in presenting the negative aspects of Behavioral Capitalism in an outstanding way. A real pioneer work. A systematic portrayal of a new variety of capitalism was probably never its own end, but only a means to an end to express the warning of the dangers of a new era of collective individualism.

The model of Behavioral Capitalism offers a systematic description and classification that can serve as a broad basis for discussion.

This paper is available under DOI 10.13140/RG.2.2.28837.65764 and has been published in the same form several times in German and English and released for discussion.

References

Zuboff, Shoshana, The Age of Surveillance Capitalism. Campus Publishing House 4 October 2018; 04 October 2018

Herteux, Andreas, Behavioral Capitalism - A New Variety of Capitalism Gains Power and Influence, DOI 10.13140/RG.2.2.18058.62402, August 2019

Herteux Andreas, Concept of the Change of Times

Herteux Andreas, The Reiz Society

Interview in "Friday" from 02.04.2019; https://www.freitag.de/autoren/the-guardian/tyrannei-die-sich-von-menschen-ernaehrt

Interview with the Süddeutsche Zeitung of 07.11.2018; https://www.sueddeutsche.de/digital/shoshana-zuboff-ueberwachungskapitalismus-google-facebook-1.4198835

Questions and answers

The model of Behavioral Capitalism has so far been positively received and has not been questioned as a form of representation and description.

Questions and discussions arose primarily for the reason that it is not normative, but merely descriptive.[26]

It wants to present mechanisms and point out challenges and opportunities. While the first two elements were considered benevolent and supportive, there were voices that denied Behavioral Capitalism positive aspects beyond the profit of the respective provider.

---

[26] However, the descriptive presentation was precisely the goal: to confront a new phenomenon, often negligently ignored, and to present it objectively in its mechanisms, in order to facilitate a discussion that does not exclude one side from it in general.

This point therefore plays an important role in the complementary questions:

Behavioral Capitalism has only negative sides and is a product of capitalist exploitation?

Behavioral Capitalism contains great dangers. These undoubtedly include the possibilities of manipulation and control. These are still massively strengthened by the conditioning of humans on small and fast stimuli since the 2nd World War, why we speak today of a homo stimulus.[27]

---

[27] In this regard, reference is made to the "Theory of the irritable society". It is a development that has been conditioned step by step by capitalism, social change and politics, without aspiring to them. The homo stimulus, the human being conditioned to short and fast stimuli, is ultimately the end product.
This more rapid stimulus reaction can be found in all milieus, as it has been established over decades both in the world of work and in the private sphere and has increased more and more. If one wants to point to an extreme, a simple subway ride is recommended and one should simply pay attention to the influence that smartphones, for example, have on the

Democracy and freedom are therefore also at stake. These dangers must be clearly identified, discussed and countered.

Nevertheless, there are also positive sides[28]. These are to be seen in the areas of the recognition of needs and their satisfaction, because through the methods of Behavioral Capitalism both known and hitherto hidden needs of the individual can be identified and satisfied.

Let's take an example. A user has so far been shaped by a direct village environment and has never got beyond it. He is not really satisfied with that, but in the end his imprint only knows this little world. Through the use of the Internet, he is now entering the world

____

lives of many people and think back to what it was like 10 years ago. With such an observation it is probably easier to understand the homo stimulus than with all grey theory.

[28] The standard argument of the technology companies that every user is rewarded with services for tapping the behaviour or the data is not to be further deepened here. The argument can certainly be discussed controversially.

of social media. Here he links to a few people who have long since moved away from the village and looks at their holiday photos one beautiful day. He likes the places and researches more about a search engine. Suddenly, the social medium and the search engine offer him more and more news and advertisements that focus on the topic of travel. The topic becomes more and more interesting and the more he searches for it, the more he becomes embedded. In the meantime he has looked at many destinations and offers, ordered travel guides and is active in a forum. He is now operating in a world of his own, in which a new longing takes centre stage, which is fuelled by the learning machine. He realizes that his previous dissatisfaction is also due to the fact that he wanted to break out of his familiar environment and see the world. So far, however, he has lacked inspiration. This is now worked out by the behavioral capitalist process, which of course immediately makes him corresponding offers of satisfaction. In the coming year, the user will go on a trip around the world.

Was he manipulated in this example? Or was it simply a wish that had previously been buried because one's own environment could not develop it together with the user? And is it really negative when this happens? As we can see, we must therefore really differentiate very precisely.

The positive sides that are described are in the end only the seduction to consume, right?

Let us stick to the concrete case of the coming holidaymaker. It is true that he will also consume many a behavioral capitalist will benefit from it. Yeah, is consumption what he wants? Or rather a form of self-development?

Isn't it precisely the actual success model of the big behavior capitalists that they adapt to individual desires and make an undreamt-of contribution to personal self-realization? A simple worker now has the chance to be heard in the social medium. To show yourself. To live out one's own interests. Maybe even being a star. When before was that ever possible? What's real?

Isn't it also about development opportunities? Ultimately, Behavioral Capitalism creates an individualized world according to the needs of the respective user and this has nothing to do with material consumption.

Those who really want to draw the debate on this simple explanatory model of the seduced consumer, have not understood the human needs and thus the human being.

In addition, an overall view is indispensable, because Behavioral Capitalism does not stand alone. Of course he, as well as the stimulus society and the homo stimulus formed by it, belong to the coming age of collective individualism, which is ultimately only slowed down by milieu struggles. And this new era is inevitable if we are not to refuse technological development. But we can decide how we want to design them.

No thinking person would exchange freedom and democracy for need recognition and satisfaction?

The question implies that people represent a homogeneous mass that all share the same attitudes and lifestyles. In fact, however, global societies disintegrate into numerous milieus, some of which have completely different values. This fragmentation of the environment is not yet complete and will continue.

This also means, however, that a part of these realities would have no problems whatsoever with, for example, exchanging one's own democratic co-determination for a guaranteed satisfaction of needs. As horrified as some members of one milieu or another may look at this statement, it does not change its truthfulness.

There are therefore also profiteers of the system and they are to be found not only among the behavioural capitalists, but above all among those for whom what seems to be in danger is worth far less or nothing at all than for others.

How can you fight this when some have all the power in their hands and half of the others are bribed?

Through new ideas and impulses such as the Model of Alternative Hegemony (AH Model). In this, a market participant is created that is under democratic control and changes or corrects capitalism from within. Through democratically controlled market power. This makes values a production factor and thus a counterweight to the influence of private corporations and the power of the state. Nor does he educate people, but companies and state entities.

For example, in order to obtain a license for a technology whose rights are held by the AH Fund, the contract of use for the company in question contains the obligation to

- fair wages

- adequate working conditions

- Compliance with environmental regulations

- and that worldwide

- transparency obligations

The company will not be forced to accept these conditions. But if it wants to generate maximum profit, it will do so. Or face the competition. It'll probably lose him. In this way, values become a factor of production and capitalism receives a new direction.

In the long run, the AH fund also makes gains, which can flow back into the countries, e.g. to support the social funds.

Of course, the model cannot be presented here in its full breadth, so please refer to separate publications.

The Alternative Hegemony Model (AH Model)

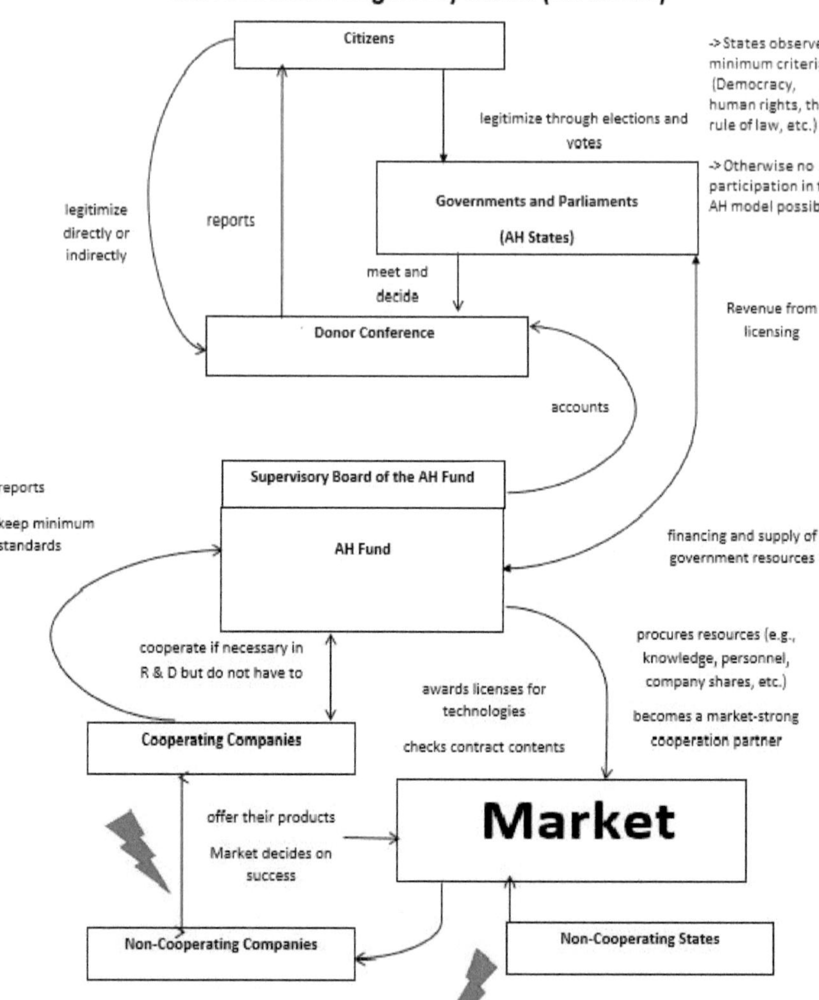

Pressure from the market or the desire for profit maximization makes it attractive to become an AH company

→ creating better conditions for workers

→ In the market, the one who adheres to these minimum standards prevails

Limited access to specific technologies or products

Market pressure makes desire for participation in the AH Fund attractive

→ Compliance with minimum standards is mandatory

→ Improvement of the life of the citizens

→ Abolition of authoritarian system

The Model of Alternative Hegemony (AH Model) sounds very good on paper, but how do you intend to force the behavioural capitalists, who are oligopolies after all, to participate?

We are in a time change that can be defined in this way:

The term "time change" is understood to mean a period of time in which its individual elements influence each other dynamically in such a way that they can bring about a reordering of the previous (global) power relations. "

These elements are:

- Technological progress

- The rise of new competitors in world markets

- Weakness of the dominant elements so far

- environmental change

- Missing Perspectives of a Part of Humanity

The pressure is therefore already there and it will constantly become stronger and the capitalists, who seem a little like a homogeneous troop to you, do not exist at all. On the contrary, there will be huge clashes between Western and controlled capitalism, where the last one seems to have the better cards at the moment.

So anyone who thinks of Google, Facebook and Co. when it comes to Behavioral Capitalism does not yet know the market power of Tencent, Baidu or Alibaba, which are much more advanced in some areas (e.g. payment systems). Apps like Tictoc or Zao are Chinese and their growth is gigantic. The western product would not necessarily win the comparison between WhatsApp and WeChat. The same applies at the state level, where Chinese expansion is unmistakable. The West will therefore come under more and more pressure and will have to consider alternatives. This in turn would be an opportunity for a model like that of Alternative Hegemony.

About the publisher

Erich von Werner Society

Birkenfelder road 3

97842 Karbach

<u>Hompage:</u>

https://www.understandandchange.com

<u>Email:</u>

erichvonwernersociety@understandand-
change.com

Facebook:

<u>https://www.facebook.com/Erich-von-Werner-
Society-Understand-and-change-353251871900615</u>

Twitter:

<u>https://twitter.com/von_society</u>

Erich von Werner Verlag

Birkenfelder road 3

97842 Karbach

Hompage:

https://www.erichvonwernerverlag.de/

Email:

Info@erichvonwernerverlag.de

Facebook:

https://de-de.facebook.com/erichvonwernerver-
lag

About the author

Andreas Herteux

<u>Hompage:</u>

https://www.andreasherteux.com/

Facebook:

https://www.facebook.com/AndreasHerteux

Twitter:

https://twitter.com/aherteuxautor